Saving Our World

# CLIMATE CHANGE

Amanda Bishop

**Marshall Cavendish** Benchmark
New York

Marshall Cavendish Benchmark
99 White Plains Road
Tarrytown, NY 10591
www.marshallcavendish.us

**Library of Congress Cataloging-in-Publication Data**

Bishop, Amanda.

   Climate change / by Amanda Bishop.

   p. cm. -- (Saving our world)

   Includes bibliographical references and index.

   ISBN 978-0-7614-3219-7

1.  Climatic changes--Juvenile literature.

2.  Global warming--Juvenile literature.

3.  Environmentalism--Juvenile literature. I. Title.

   QC981.8.C5B56 2009

   551.6--dc22

   2008014553

The photographs in this book are used by permission and through the courtesy of:

Half Title: Samuel Acosta / Shutterstock

Stevegeer / Istockphoto: 4-5, Chad Ehlers / Photolibrary: 6-7, Andre Nantel / Shutterstock: 8-9, FotoliaComp_3014607: 10-11, Dan Collier / Shutterstock: 12-13, Lidian Neeleman / Dreamstime: 12b, Vera Bogaerts /Shutterstock: 14-15, NASA: 17, Samuel Acosta / Shutterstock: 18-19, Associated Press: 21, Associated Press: 23,

Associated Press: 24, 200296557-008: 26,

Cover photo: Dan Guravich / Photo Researchers / Photolibrary: Fouquin/Shutterstock: Oleg Prikhodko/ Istockphoto.

Created by: Q2A Media

Creative Director: Simmi Sikka

Series Editor: Maura Christopher

Series Art Director: Sudakshina Basu

Series Designers: Dibakar Acharjee, Joita Das, Mansi Mittal, Rati Mathur and Shruti Bahl

Series Illustrator: Abhideep Jha and Ajay Sharma

Photo research by Sejal Sehgal

Series Project Managers: Ravneet Kaur and Shekhar Kapur

Printed in Malaysia

1 3 5 6 4 2

# CONTENTS

# Climate Change

During the past few years, most of the world's scientists have come to agree that Earth's climate is changing. Climate is made up of temperature, precipitation, and wind patterns in an area over a long period of time.

## Natural Changes

**Climate** changes naturally. For instance, the last **ice age** ended about eighteen thousand years ago. During the ice age, massive ice sheets called **glaciers** covered much of North America. Since then, the climate has changed a great deal. Natural climate change takes place over very long periods of time. In the short term, however, climates are usually steady and predictable. The climate change has been observed during the past 150 years. Scientists believe that human activity is causing the current climate to change much faster than it would naturally.

*Climate change is a worldwide phenomenon of changing temperatures, **precipitation**, and weather events, such as storms.*

# Climate Change and Global Warming

The **atmosphere** is made up of the air we breathe, along with many other gases. These gases help control the temperature near the Earth's surface. Today, people's activity affects the **composition** of the atmosphere. The changes we make to the atmosphere cause a phenomenon known as **global warming**. Global warming is the slow increase of Earth's average temperature. The rising average temperature affects climates all over the world.

## QUESTION TIME

### What is the relationship between climate and weather?

Weather is the combination of temperature, wind, and precipitation in a specific place at a specific time. Climate is made up of weather patterns over a long period of time.

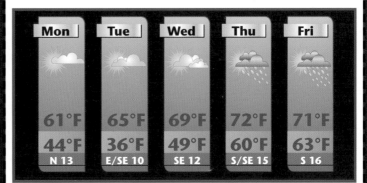

| Mon | Tue | Wed | Thu | Fri |
|-----|-----|-----|-----|-----|
| 61°F | 65°F | 69°F | 72°F | 71°F |
| 44°F | 36°F | 49°F | 60°F | 63°F |
| N 13 | E/SE 10 | SE 12 | S/SE 15 | S 16 |

*Daily weather forecasts such as this one show local weather conditions including temperature and rainfall.*

# The Great Debate

Scientists first began studying global warming in the early 1900s. By the 1970s, experts had gathered enough information to suggest that the climate was changing rapidly. Yet people resisted the idea that humans had anything to do with a change in climate. Some scientists maintained that the changes were the result of a natural cycle. Many people did not believe that climate change was happening at all. Scientists continued to collect evidence through the 1980s and 1990s. By then, people had experienced several of the hottest years on record. Today, most people accept that climate change requires urgent attention.

*Climate change can affect farming and food production.*

## Why Does Climate Change Matter?

Climate affects people, animals, and plants. When weather patterns shift, plants may die because they are too hot or too cold. They may dry up from a lack of water, or die under a flood. If weather patterns are unpredictable, people face challenges. They may be unable to grow food locally. Their shelters may no longer be suitable. They may be forced to move in order to find enough resources to survive.

## EYE-OPENER

Climatologists are scientists who study climate. They study information about climates from hundreds of thousands of years ago. They collect ice cores, or tubes of ice, that are drilled out of glaciers. Tiny air bubbles are trapped in the ice. Climatologists examine the air in the bubbles to find information about climates in different time periods.

# The Carbon Cycle

Carbon is an element that is found in the atmosphere, on land, and in the ocean. There is carbon in every living thing, too. Almost 20 percent of each human body is made up of carbon.

## Cycling Carbon

The **carbon** cycle is a process that moves carbon between the land, the air, and the sea. Under normal conditions, the carbon cycle keeps itself in balance. During the cycle, carbon is absorbed, stored, and released in different forms. Stored carbon is tied up in **carbon sinks**. Carbon sinks store carbon because they absorb more carbon than they release.

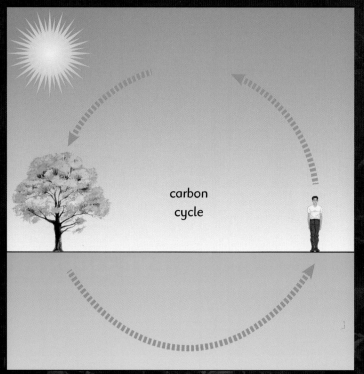

carbon cycle

*Humans breathe out carbon dioxide. Plants take in carbon dioxide.*

However, changing conditions can release carbon stored in a carbon sink. For example, a forest is a carbon sink because the trees, plants, and soil all contain large amounts of carbon. When a forest is cleared, in a process called **deforestation**, all of the stored carbon is released into the atmosphere. Soil stores large amounts of carbon when it is cold or frozen, as in **permafrost**. When the soil warms up, however, the carbon is released.

*Plants take in **carbon dioxide** and release oxygen.*

## QUESTION TIME ?

### How is carbon released naturally into the atmosphere?

Plants **respire**, or release, carbon dioxide, just as humans exhale carbon dioxide. Tiny organisms called **decomposers** release carbon dioxide as they break down dead plants and animals. Carbon stored in trees is released when the wood is burned. Volcanic eruptions release carbon from deep inside the Earth's crust.

## Carbon on the Loose

Over the past two hundred years, humans have released more stored carbon than in all of history before then. Most of the carbon we have released has come from forests and **fossil fuels**, such as **oil**, **coal**, and **natural gas**. When forests are cleared for farming and development, the carbon stored there is released into the atmosphere. Once the trees are gone, they can no longer absorb carbon dioxide from the atmosphere. Fossil fuels are the ancient remains of plants and animals that are stored deep in the Earth. When fossil fuels are burned, the carbon stored in them is released.

## So What?

The excess of carbon dioxide in the atmosphere is throwing the carbon cycle out of balance. Carbon dioxide is one of the greenhouse gases. Greenhouse gases trap the Sun's heat close to the Earth's surface, causing temperatures to rise. Warm temperatures make the air better able to hold water vapor, which is another greenhouse gas. As greenhouse gases accumulate in the atmosphere, the temperature rises. As the temperature rises, the atmosphere builds up greenhouse gases. This phenomenon is known as a **positive feedback loop**. A positive feedback loop is a cycle in which an action, A, has a result, B, which makes it more likely for A to happen again. When A happens again, B results again. A loop is created as a result of the positive feedback between A and B.

*In this century, the use of fossil fuels as a source of energy for electricity and transportation has led to huge amounts of carbon dioxide being released into the atmosphere.*

## QUESTION TIME ?

### What are the greenhouse gases?

Carbon dioxide, water vapor, methane, nitrous oxide, and chlorofluorocarbons (CFCs) are all greenhouse gases.

# The Greenhouse Effect

**People use greenhouses to grow plants. In a greenhouse, clear panels of glass allow light and heat energy from the Sun to travel in. The panels stop heat from escaping.**

## Greenhouse Gases in Action

The **greenhouse effect** is a term used to describe how heat energy is trapped near the Earth's surface. The gases that make up the atmosphere, including oxygen, carbon dioxide, and several other gases, allow light and heat energy from the sun to reach the planet's surface. They do not allow the heat energy to escape. Without the greenhouse effect, our planet would be much colder.

## Off Balance

The greenhouse effect happens naturally. However, in the past two hundred years, people have added more greenhouse gases to the atmosphere than in all of human history. Adding these gases has thrown off the balance in the atmosphere. As a result, the greenhouse effect is not just keeping Earth warm—it is warming up the Earth. The greenhouse effect is the main cause of global warming.

*Heat builds in a greenhouse almost as soon as the Sun starts shining, so plants stay warm even when it is cold outside.*

*The greenhouse effect has kept the temperature on Earth in balance for thousands of years. Our actions are changing the balance. As the greenhouse effect grows stronger the planet gets warmer.*

## QUESTION TIME ?

### How quickly is the Earth warming?

Scientists believe that the average global temperature has increased by one degree over the past hundred years. However, based on data from the past few decades, scientists predict that the planet could warm by 2.5–11 degrees Fahrenheit (1.4–6 degrees Celsius) by the end of the century.

# Life at the Poles

The Arctic, also called the North Pole, is home to many unique species of plants and animals, such as polar bears. Antarctica, or the South Pole, is the coldest, driest continent. Antarctica's glaciers and waters are home to wildlife such as penguins.

## Melting Ice

Rising temperatures are causing ice sheets and sea ice to melt. The melting ice creates a positive feedback loop. White ice and snow reflect light, which means that they do not trap heat. As ice melts, the land or dark water underneath the ice is exposed to sunlight. The dark surface absorbs light and holds heat. As the surface grows warmer, the heat melts more ice. When the ice melts, even more land or dark water is exposed, which leads to more melting ice, and so on.

## QUESTION TIME ?

### Where does melted sea ice go?

Melted sea ice becomes fresh water that runs into the oceans. Sea levels have been steady for about eight thousand years. Now scientists predict that melting sea ice is adding so much water to the oceans that sea levels may rise as much as 10 to 20 feet (3–6 m) in the next two hundred years.

# Polar Life Depends on Ice

In the Artic and Antarctica, tiny plants called **phytoplankton** require sea ice to live. The phytoplankton are eaten by small animals called **krill**. Krill are eaten by many animals, including penguins and seals in the Antarctic and narwhals in the Arctic. As sea ice melts, the numbers of plankton and krill are reduced. The animals that feed on them lose their food source, and may die out.

*About four million people live in the Arctic. Changes to the environment affect their homes, work, and lifestyles.*

15

# What about Weather?

Changes to the climate result in changes to local weather patterns. Some places may become warmer, while others become cooler. Precipitation may increase or decrease, making some places wetter and others much drier.

## Storm Watch

Many scientists believe that climate change will lead to an increase of extreme weather events such as tropical storms, hurricanes, winter storms, flooding, and **droughts.** The late 1990s and the early 2000s saw many powerful hurricanes, including the first hurricane ever to occur in the south Atlantic Ocean. Hurricanes can cause severe damage to coastal communities, destroying homes and coastlines. Many hurricanes are followed by floods. Floods occur when waves and rainwater hit the ground faster than the ground can absorb the water.

## EYE-OPENER

Many of the hottest years on record have been recorded in the past fifteen years. In some places, higher temperatures have resulted in periods of extreme lasting heat called **heat waves**. A heat wave in Europe during the summer of 2003 resulted in more than twenty-five thousand deaths.

*This image shows the places where temperatures were 18 degrees Farhenheit (10 degrees Celsius) hotter in 2003 than in 2001.*

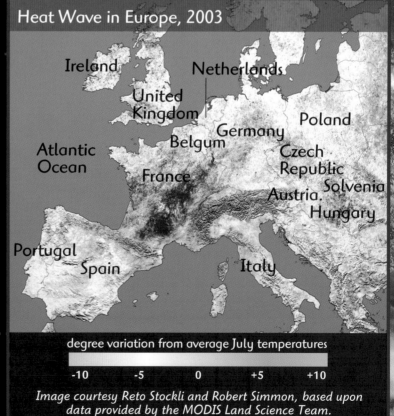

Heat Wave in Europe, 2003

degree variation from average July temperatures

-10    -5    0    +5    +10

*Image courtesy Reto Stockli and Robert Simmon, based upon data provided by the MODIS Land Science Team.*

Storm patterns may change with the
climate. Places that have never experienced
tornadoes may be at risk from them.

# Changing Habitats

Ecosystems are made up of plants and animals that live together in a habitat, or home. When weather patterns change, ecosystems may also be changed, affecting plants, animals, and their habitats.

## Rising Temperatures

Every plant needs a certain amount of warmth, sunlight, and rainfall to grow. Changes in weather conditions can leave plants too cool, too warm, too damp, or too dry to survive. Many animals rely on plants for food. When plants cannot survive, these animals must find other types of food or die. They may need to find new **habitats.**

## QUESTION TIME ?

### What is coral bleaching?

Coral reefs are among the most colorful, diverse, and important habitats on Earth, but they are in serious danger because of global warming. The coral that make up the reefs depend on a type of **algae**, a tiny plant, for food. Warming water temperatures prevent the algae from growing. Without the algae, coral starve to death. Dead coral lose their vibrant colors. This is called coral bleaching.

## On the Move

Loss of suitable habitat is one of the biggest dangers to animals today. Animals that can no longer live in their habitat must **invade**, or move into, another habitat. Once there, they may compete with other animals for food. If the new animals are more successful at finding food, other animals may die out. These other animals are important to their **ecosystem**, so the ecosystem changes when they are lost. New animals may also carry diseases to new areas. Currently, many species of animals in North America are moving northward to cooler temperatures. Grizzly bears are moving into polar bear habitat, and red foxes are moving into arctic fox habitat. These animals change ecosystems as they relocate.

*Loss of habitat threatens many types of plants and animals.*

# Climate and People

**Sudden cold snaps, heat waves, flooding, droughts, and windstorms can mean that places where food now grows well become unable to grow food. The result of food shortages could be widespread hunger among many people.**

## Trouble on the Coasts

Millions of people make their homes on islands or along the coasts of oceans. Many of these places have a high **population density**, which means that a large number of people live in a small area. Rising sea levels and extreme weather events such as hurricanes and tropical storms can destroy homes and **contaminate**, or ruin, fresh water supplies. It can also reduce the usable land along the coast.

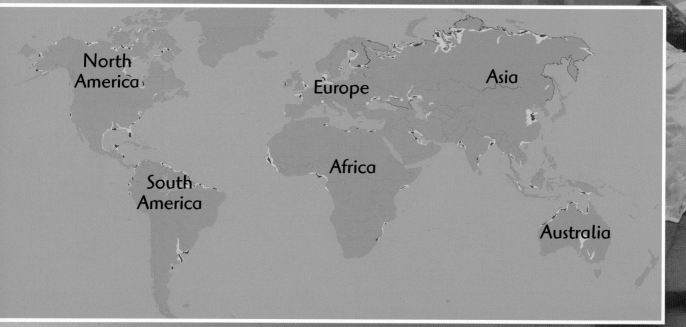

North America

Europe

Asia

South America

Africa

Australia

Regions Vulnerable to Sea Level Rise

Global warming may mean that there is not enough clean, fresh water for everyone to drink. Mountain snow melts each spring, adding water to rivers and streams. When warm temperatures reduce snow and ice on mountain tops, there is less snow to melt. Many countries depend on mountain streams for fresh water.

*Large numbers of people may be displaced, or forced to move because of rising sea levels. Displaced people will have to find new places to live and work.*

# Politics and Action

Climate change is a global problem. The gases in the atmosphere and the water in the oceans move around, the whole planet. As a result, the effects of climate change will be felt worldwide.

## Coming to an Agreement

When thinking about reducing greenhouse gases, political leaders have to weigh the concerns of scientists, citizens, and industries. Some people argue that the **developed countries** should be responsible for reducing greenhouse gases. Other people argue that **developing countries** must help prevent the problem from growing worse.

## The Kyoto Protocol

In 1997, the international agreement known as the Kyoto Protocol was created to reduce greenhouse gases. The Kyoto Protocol officially took effect in 2005, but the United States, the biggest greenhouse gas emitter, still has not signed on. In 2007, at the Bali Climate Conference, politicians from around the world began working toward a new international agreement to address the problem of climate change.

United States of America · Russia · China · Japan · India

■ Five highest emitting countries

# united nations
# climate change conference

Nusa Dua - Bali, Indonesia, 3-14 December 2007

Governments around the world have spent many years trying to agree on what to do about climate change.

## QUESTION TIME ?

### How did scientists prove that action needed to be taken?

In 1988, a group of two thousand scientists from 130 countries was formed to study climate change. Their reports have urged the countries of the world to take immediate action on climate change.

# Making a Difference

Believe it or not, everyone can help prevent climate change. Each person on the planet makes decisions every day that can help the environment. The first step—knowing about the problem—is the toughest one.

## Alternative Fuels

Many scientists are working on alternative sources of energy. Renewable energy sources, such as wind power and solar power, do not release greenhouse gases. Scientists have also developed many alternative sources of fuel. **Hybrid** cars use a combination of fossil fuel and electricity from a rechargeable battery. **Biofuels**, such as **biodiesel** or **ethanol**, are made of natural materials that produce fewer greenhouse gases than fossil fuels. Many cities around the world have introduced biofuel vehicles into the public transit system to help reduce greenhouse gases, and cities such as Knoxville, Tennessee, are increasing their use of biodiesel in public transit.

*Learn as much as you can about climate change, its effects, and how people are trying to make a difference.*

## What Is a Carbon Footprint?

You may have heard people talk about carbon footprints. Your carbon footprint is a measure of how much greenhouse gas your actions put into the atmosphere. In order to know what your carbon footprint is, you have to determine your family's **emission**, or release, of greenhouse gases. This is based on your heating and cooling levels, travel, and use of electricity. There are several carbon footprint calculators available online to help you and your family make the calculations. Once you have determined your household's carbon footprint, you can find ways to reduce your emissions.

# Reducing Fossil Fuels

Almost all of the energy in the United States—about 86 percent—comes from burning fossil fuels. Cars, boats, buses, trucks, airplanes, ships, and some power plants burn a great deal of fossil fuel.

Buying local food and goods is a great way to reduce emissions. Shipping food and goods across the state, country, or continent requires a lot of fossil fuel. When you buy produce from local farmers, you are buying food that did not require much fossil fuel to get to you.

## Fuel Efficiency

Fuel efficiency is fuel use that wastes as little energy as possible so that less fuel is burned overall. Small cars and new cars are usually more fuel-efficient than large and old cars. If your family has more than one vehicle, try to use the most fuel-efficient one whenever possible. Keep extra weight out of the car and make sure that tires are properly inflated to keep the car running efficiently. When shopping for a new car, encourage your parents to find the smallest vehicle that meets their needs. They may also want to consider buying a hybrid car, or another car that runs on an alternative fuel.

*Organize a walking or biking group to travel to and from school with friends to cut down on the number of cars on the road.*

# Energy Overuse

Wise energy use at home and at school can help reduce your greenhouse gas emissions. By conserving electricity, you can help fight climate change.

## Conserve at Home

Almost every home can be more energy efficient. To conserve energy, use less electricity by turning out the lights when leaving a room and turning off or unplugging the television, computer, and game system when not in use. Avoid using energy to heat water by taking short showers instead of long baths, and wash clothes in cold water. Keep the temperature in your house at 68 degrees Fahrenheit (20 degrees Celsius) in winter and 77 degrees Fahrenheit (25 degrees Celsius) in summer.

*Be creative in your efforts to reduce emissions. Remember that every single reduction counts!*

## Consume Less

We are all **consumers**. We buy goods such as prepackaged food, clothing, and electronics and consume, or use, them. Think about the amount of fossil fuels that are burned to make and package goods and distribute them to consumers. You can consume less by minimizing waste and reusing items whenever possible. Look for items that have no unnecessary packaging. Carry a reusable bag when you shop. Look at labels to find products made close to home. Find out if there are any alternatives to buying new things, such as borrowing, renting, sharing, or buying used items.

# Glossary

**algae:** Simple aquatic plants.

**atmosphere:** The combination of gases that make up the air near the Earth's surface.

**biodiesel:** A biofuel that can substitute for diesel.

**biofuel:** Fuel made from a living thing, such as a plant.

**carbon:** An element that is basic to all life.

**carbon dioxide:** The gas form of carbon.

**carbon sinks:** Places where carbon is stored naturally, such as trees or swamps.

**climate:** The weather patterns in a place over a long period of time.

**coal:** A fossil fuel made of ancient plants.

**composition:** The makeup of an object.

**consumer:** An individual who uses, eats, or buys goods.

**contaminate:** To make something impure or unsuitable by adding something else to it.

**decomposer:** An organism that breaks down organic matter.

**deforestation:** The process by which forests are burned or cut down.

**developed countries:** Countries that have developed economies.

**developing countries:** Countries that are working to develop their economies.

**drought:** A prolonged period of dry weather due to lack of rainfall.

**ecosystem:** A system of plants, animals, and habitat that supports itself.

**element:** A basic chemical that cannot be broken down further.

**emission:** The release of a gas.

**ethanol:** A biofuel made from corn.

**fossil fuels:** Fuels that are drilled from the Earth and made of the remains of ancient living things.

**glacier:** A massive sheet of ice.

**global warming:** The process by which the average temperature on the Earth's surface is slowly rising.

**greenhouse effect:** The effect of greenhouse gases in the atmosphere that trap heat near the Earth's surface and raise the temperature.

**habitat:** The location and conditions in which a plant or animal lives.

**heat wave:** A prolonged period of hot weather.

**hybrid:** Describes a car that uses both fossil fuel and electricity to run.

**ice age:** A period in the history of the Earth in which glaciers covered much of the Earth's surface.

**invade:** To move into the territory or habitat of another.

**krill:** A tiny marine animal.

**natural gas:** A fossil fuel.

**oil:** A fossil fuel used to make gasoline.

**permafrost:** The layer of permanently frozen soil in the Arctic.

**phytoplankton:** Microscopic plants.

**population density:** A measurement of how many people live in a given area.

**positive feedback loop:** A series of actions that occur in succession over and over.

**precipitation:** The water that falls to the Earth as rain, snow, hail, or sleet.

**respire:** To carry out respiration, or the intake and release of gases.

# Find Out More

- http://epa.gov/climatechange/kids/index.html. This site, sponsored by the Environmental Protection Agency, has plenty of information about climate change, the greenhouse effect, and how kids can help make a difference.

- http://www.davidsuzuki.org/kids/. Take David Suzuki's Nature Challenge to help reduce the Greenhouse Effect! This site has plenty of useful information that will help you think more carefully about the decisions you make.

- http://unep.org/tunza/children/. The home page for the United Nations Environment Programme has stories, contests, and great tips for helping the environment for kids all over the world.

- http://www.dnr.state.wi.us/org/caer/ce/eek/earth/air/global.htm. The Department of Natural Resources in Wisconsin hosts this site. It answers some questions about global warming, and it has links to other environmental topics, too.

- http://www.zerofootprintkids.com/kids_home.aspx. This simple carbon footprint calculator can help you find out what your carbon footprint is. It will show you your impact on carbon, land, and water, and help you compare your resource use to national averages around the world.

- www.epa.gov/climatechange/emissions/ind_calculator.html

# Index